Portraits of the Iron Horse

THE AMERICAN LOCOMOTIVE IN PICTURES AND STORY

Drawings by OTTO KUHLER

Story by Robert S. Henry

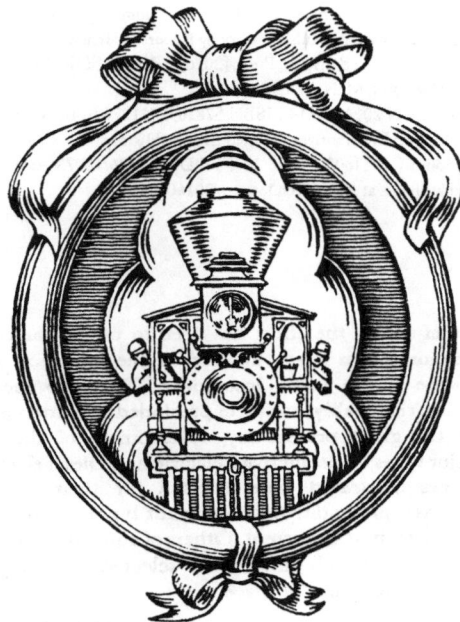

SUNSTONE PRESS

SANTA FE

Library of Congress Cataloging-in-Publication Data
Names: Henry, Robert Selph, 1889-1970, author. | Kuhler, Otto, 1894-1977,
  illustrator.
Title: Portraits of the iron horse : the American locomotive in pictures and
  story / drawings by Otto Kuhler ; story by Robert S. Henry.
Description: Santa Fe : Sunstone Press, [2016] | Reprint of the 1937 ed.
  published by Rand, McNally, Chicago.
Identifiers: LCCN 2016014114 | ISBN 9781632931276 (softcover : alk. paper)
Subjects: LCSH: Locomotives--United States--History.
Classification: LCC TJ603.2 .H46 2016 | DDC 625.26/10973--dc23
LC record available at http://lccn.loc.gov/2016014114

In this brief survey the effort has been to present as complete a panorama as space allowed of the evolution and present state of the steam locomotive. To make such a presentation reasonably complete precluded any attempt to illustrate the great present-day development of the two other major types of locomotives, electric and Diesel electric. Locomotives illustrated were selected for their historic interest, or as representative of important types of American railroad power, past or present. Others of equal interest and importance might well have been selected—but, again, there are the limitations of space.

OTTO KUHLER
ROBERT S. HENRY

Manufactured in the United States of America

INTRODUCTION

Portraits of the Iron Horse is the first book designed exclusively for rail fans over half-a-century ago, and Sunstone Press, with the advice and help of Otto Kuhler, the only surviving member of the original author team, is proud to present an unabridged reprint of this highly treasured collector's item.

To recreate the early experiences surrounding the first publication, we asked Mr. Kuhler to tell us some of the adventures he and the other young Iron Horse enthusiasts had in calling attention to their "pet" and, in finally giving it its rightful place in American journalistic history.

"The garishly-decorated trains of early days were national heroes in one sense. They were honored, feated, met at every station like royalty!" But, in spite of their early glamour and their tremendous impact on the Nation's economy and culture, Otto noted, they were soon taken for granted.

As he recalls, "It took the ruinous depression of the 30's, as well as the threat of other upstarts in the transportation business, the automobile and the airplane, to awake the consciousness of three visionaries, each of them loosely connected with railroading." The three were eventually responsible for the publication of *Portraits of the Iron Horse.*

To jog the public consciousness, these men who had met by accident, "unanimously selected the arts of word and picture to portray the historic drama and hidden romance of the Iron Horse." There is no doubt that they did, indeed, raise the train to a preeminent position, beloved by young and old.

But we'll let Otto tell the story.

"When Robert M. Van Sant, genial editor of the *Baltimore and Ohio Magazine,* engaged me as its designer at $15 per month, he included a pass 'over the lines' to contact rail officials, as well as equipment builders, with aggressive new thoughts for revival of their enterprises. Last to join us was the brilliant historian of the Civil War, Colonel Robert S. Henry, representing, as a vice president, the then sharply economizing Association of American Railroads in Washington.

"With our personal incomes reduced to near starvation proportions, and with our savings gone, united enthusiasm nevertheless, brought about the momentum needed to stimulate public opinion and to justify continued efforts to glorify our beloved "pet," the Iron Horse. To catch the attention of youth, Van Sant had built a folding art gallery made up of a collection of full color train paintings from my personal collection. With business at a standstill, I had found ample time to paint after the chores at our farm were done.

"The collection was set up in stations where thousands of school children were invited to see the paintings. (Vandalism, happily, was still unknown.)

"Then one day I traveled by coach with a shoebox lunch packed for me by my wife, Simonne, to retrieve my paintings from the last exhibition in Chicago. I was met by a deeply disappointed friend, Colonel Henry. He had just had his book about trains, illustrated with black and white photos, turned down. The publisher wanted color illustrations. 'Is *That* all?' I said. And though we had only a brief time on the train while engines were changed in Akron, in those fateful 10 minutes of engine change, the first illustrated railroad book honoring railroad history was born — in full color!''

Armed with some 30 of Otto Kuhler's paintings, the men jumped off the train and returned to Saalfield Publishing Company, publisher of Shirley Temple 10¢ children's books, which eventually published and sold thousands of *On The Railroad* paperback books through the five-and-dime stores. ''This,'' remarked Otto, ''really laid the foundation for the voluminous present day nostalgia-bolstered railroad literature of 50 years ago.''

Encouraged by the substantial revenue received, Henry and Kuhler traveled to entertain Railroad Clubs with illustrated lectures on glass lantern slides they had prepared and paid for out of their own pockets. No effort was too great for their ''pet.''

''From the very beginning,'' Otto said, ''the developing steam locomotive had caught the public's imagination. It had a high profile even before the invention of photography and during a time when printed illustrations were very scarce and costly.''

When Kuhler hit upon the idea of combining locomotive history into one illustrated volume, Colonel Henry, with the extensive library of the Association of American Railroads readily available to him, wrote the story, furnishing Kuhler with old woodcuts or hand-engraved illustrations. The artist skillfully gave old and newer engines the correct historical and natural landscape settings in which they functioned. The mechanical detail was faultless. It took the artist several years to produce close to a hundred drawings, in a distinctly new art technique of his own invention called ''dry brush'' drawing. He often worked late into the night by a Kerosene lamp, he recalls, ''since due to lack of funds the electricity had been cut off!''

Rand McNally, printers and publishers of Rail Road timetables and stationery (and much later, the famed roadmaps for motorists), offered to publish the work of the three railroad enthusiasts in a deluxe edition, to be designed and illustrated by Kuhler. The authors were overly modest. They limited the first printing of *Portraits Of The Iron Horse* to a mere 250 copies.

We feel far more confident than they!

Jody Ellis, President
Sunstone Press

CONTENTS

ILLUSTRATIONS

THE "BEST FRIEND OF CHARLESTON"

This, the first American locomotive built for and used in regular service, ran on the South Carolina Railroad, now part of the Southern Railway, in 1830 and 1831. Designed by E. L. Miller and C. E. Detmold, a merchant and a machinist of Charleston, it was good enough to pull a "brigade of cars" at thirty-five miles an hour. Before the "Best Friend" two experimental engines were built in the United States—the steam-driven car which Colonel John Stevens drove around a track on his Hoboken estate, and the tiny "Tom Thumb" which Peter Cooper ran on the Baltimore & Ohio. Still another locomotive ran in the United States before 1830—the "Stourbridge Lion" which Horatio Allen brought from England and drove on the track of the Delaware and Hudson Canal Company.

8

CHAPTER I

Something New in All History

LOCOMOTIVE engines," people called them a century ago, because they were just that—engines which could move themselves. In that respect they were new.

Machinery was not new. From the days of the Pharaohs, and before, men had used machines worked by the power of muscle, or by the weight of water against the wheel, or by the push of the wind against the arms of the windmill.

Nor were engines new. The Greeks, in ancient days, had a sort of fire-heated vapor engine which mystified the populace by swinging open the doors of a temple in Alexandria. For at least a century before the invention of locomotives, clanking stationary steam engines drove the pumps that lifted water from deep mines or whirled the spindles on spinning frames.

The wheel was in use when history first began to be recorded, but then, and for thousands of years afterward, the only power to move the wheel on land was muscle power. On the water vessels were moved by the pressure of the wind against the sail, but to move men and their little loads to and from river or sea took the back-breaking, leg-weary labor of men and of animals.

By the beginning of the nineteenth century, the burden was somewhat eased here and there in England, by the building of short stretches of tramway tracks on which a horse could pull several times the load he could move on the ordinary road. But in most places and for the most part, men still moved themselves and their belongings over the land about as they had done in the days of the Pharaohs.

And then came "locomotive engines"—engines light enough to move about on wheels; strong enough to pull behind them trains of cars bearing many times the load of the strongest horse; swift enough to outstrip the fastest horse; tireless enough to open up whole continents to the use of man. The new beast of burden was called the "Iron Horse," but in the name was more of fancy than of fact. Mechanical power applied to land locomotion was not a mere improvement on the power of the horse. It was something new in all the history of mankind. With its coming a new age dawned, an age in which men, released from the toil of transporting a bare and meager subsistence, turned their powers more and more to the production of goods in increasing abundance.

Nowhere was there greater need for the work which the locomotive could do than in North America in the early nineteenth century. To open to settlement a continent so vast, so rich in every resource for production, required a sort of transportation which did not exist in the world when, in 1784, the greatest of Americans proposed to "smooth the road and make easy the way" to the West. The "West" of which George Washington spoke was the valley of the Ohio, the region just beyond the Alleghenies, then far more remote from the settlements of the Atlantic seaboard than the Pacific Coast is today.

When Washington spoke—and this was even before he was chosen President—he had in mind the only inland transportation his world knew—roads or, perhaps, canals along which horses might draw loads in creaking wagons or

10

THE "DeWITT CLINTON"

The third locomotive built for regular service, like the two earlier ones of the South Carolina Railroad, was built by the West Point Foundry in New York. It was designed by John B. Jervis—a man renowned in locomotive history. Its first run was between Albany and Schenectady, on the Mohawk & Hudson Railroad, now part of the New York Central. The purpose of the railroad was to avoid the slow and tiresome canal-boat passage of the series of locks between Schenectady and Troy, terminus of the Erie Canal. The "DeWitt Clinton" wasn't slow—it pulled five connected stagecoaches at thirty miles an hour—and from all accounts a trip behind it was anything but monotonous.

11

in gliding canal boats. But almost at the time he spoke, as far back as 1786, Oliver Evans, a Yankee mechanic, had the vision and the mechanical skill to build high-pressure steam engines. He actually built, at Philadelphia, a steam carriage with a long Latin name, the *Eruktor Amphibiolus,* which clumsily and slowly moved on land and water; and he dreamed and wrote of a day when there would be tracks on which such engines might run at speeds as high as fifteen miles an hour. But there were no tracks in America then, and very little money with which to build them, even if the people of that day had had confidence in Evans' "crazy dreams"—which they did not. Against him was not only the age-old popular idea that "it can't be done," but also the most respectable scientific opinion of the day.

Yet, if this rich continent were to be settled and civilized, there must be good and cheap transportation. Land a little distance from the natural waterways was almost worthless for lack of a way to get its products to market. And even the use of the natural waterways was uncertain and unsatisfactory, limited by ice in the winter, by low water in the summer, by floods in the spring. Canals were tried and were found useful; but canals were expensive to build, they could not be carried over the mountains, they were limited in capacity, and they suffered from being frozen up, in the northern half of the country, for nearly half the year.

Roads, for the most part, were little more than tracks cut through the forests—tracks rough and rutted, dotted with stumps and with mudholes where, during a large part of the year, wagons sank to the axle. Such transportation added enormously to the cost of moving persons and things. Only small and precious commodities could stand this cost for any distance. Moreover, such transportation kept life moving at a slow pace. The news of Washington's death in the winter of 1799 took ten days to reach Boston by

"JOHN BULL" AND HIS COWCATCHER

The "cowcatcher" was introduced to America by a British-built locomotive, the "John Bull," which came over in 1831 to become the first locomotive to run on any part of the present Pennsylvania Railroad. The "John Bull," however, did not bring the cowcatcher with it. When it arrived it had the usual square front-end of the British locomotive, which was all right in a land where railroad tracks were used only by trains, but wouldn't do where the train sometimes had to dispute its way with wandering livestock. The ingenious engineers of the Camden & Amboy, therefore, devised a cowcatcher, mounted it on an extra axle added to the front of the engine, and prepared to clear the way. This historic engine, now in the Smithsonian Institution at Washington, still can run under its own power.

13

stagecoach, and that on the best road in the country between the only large centers of population.

Improved turnpikes began to be built early in the nineteenth century. The most famous of these was the National Road, stretching westward from Baltimore across the Alleghenies. But even on this road, the best highway in America in 1827, the cost of hauling 200 pounds of freight—say, a barrel of flour—between the Ohio River and the Chesapeake Bay was $4.00—more than ten times the average cost of moving freight over the same distance by rail today.

On the common dirt roads of the day the cost was far higher. Between Jackson and Vicksburg, in Mississippi, five yoke of oxen were required to haul a load of six bales of cotton at what was almost literally a snail's pace.

The Quartermaster-General of the United States Army reported, in 1877, that transportation of the year's supplies for troops in the Department of Dakota had cost $71,590. To haul the same supplies in 1869, before the railroad came, would have cost the government six times as much, he reported—a saving due to the extension of only one line of the Northern Pacific part of the way across the vast territory which was to become the states of North Dakota and South Dakota.

Wherever the Iron Horse ran on its light tracks of iron, the cost of transportation came tumbling down. The freight rates on railroads, in 1848, averaged about seven cents for hauling one ton a mile—about a third as much as it usually cost to haul by road. By 1865 better railroads and better engines cut this average down to about three cents per ton per mile. Today the efficient modern locomotive, drawing long trains of cars on heavy steel tracks, is able to move freight faster and more securely than ever before, for an average revenue of *less than one cent a ton a mile.*

"OLD IRONSIDES"

First of the long line of engines carrying the Baldwin name plate, "Old Ironsides" was designed by Matthias Baldwin, a Philadelphia jeweler, after he had inspected carefully the English "John Bull" engine, imported in 1831 to operate on the Camden & Amboy Railroad, now part of the Pennsylvania. Baldwin's first product ran on the Philadelphia, Germantown & Norristown, now part of the Reading Railway. Its owners would not let it go out when it rained—not because they were saving its paint but because they were not sure that an engine would pull on wet rails. The first time it was caught out in a shower, that question was answered. Before it was two years old some venturesome driver, name now unknown, "let her out" to a short burst of mile-a-minute speed.

15

The first actual combination of the things it takes to make a railroad in the modern sense—that is, an engine pulling a train of cars on a track—was made in 1803 by the Cornish engineer Richard Trevithick. His pressure steam locomotive pulled a train of loaded cars uphill from the waterside to a Welsh iron furnace.

But that was not the sort of thing of which the American railroad pioneers dreamed. Oliver Evans and John Stevens saw the railroad as more than a mere connection of mine or quarry or furnace with some near-by stream. They looked far ahead to long lines of rails connecting distant cities or reaching into the remote interior.

That sort of thing was not to be in their day. But later—with the growing population impatiently pressing westward; with the increase of trade and the accumulation of wealth in the seaport cities; with the sharpening competition for business; and with the growing skill in the use of power and machinery—men gradually brought together the vision, the courage, the skill, and the capital necessary to build and operate long roads of rails to the western interior. Those men did more than build local tramways; they created systems of transportation.

In 1828 a rail line started from Baltimore westward to the waters of the Ohio; from Charleston another to tap the commerce of the uplands toward the mountains. But what was to pull the loads on these far-reaching tracks?

By this time people were beginning to talk about the railways in England and how miraculously easy they made it to get about and to transport goods. But "railroad" had not yet come generally to mean steam railroad; most people thought of a railroad as being merely a better kind of road rather than the better road plus a new kind of motive power. A writer of the day tells how, on rails, a single horse drew eight cars loaded with 200 barrels of flour a

THE "ATLANTIC"

Phineas Davis, a watchmaker of York, Pennsylvania, built the "Atlantic" more than a century ago, but it can still do a day's work. Davis' "York," which won the Baltimore & Ohio prize competition for a steam locomotive to take the place of horses in pulling trains of that railroad in 1831, started the "grasshopper" type—four-wheeled engines with vertical boilers and cylinders, burning anthracite coal and driving through "walking beams" connected to crank axles. Davis fell to his death from one of his own engines running on the new branch line to Washington, but the type survived him. These engines were in use in light service as late as the 1860's, and two of them, the "Atlantic" and the "Thomas Jefferson," are still capable of running under their own steam.

distance of six and one-half miles in forty-six minutes "with triumphant success." Indeed, the superiority of rails to common roads was so impressive that, in the eyes of many, the rails alone looked like the complete answer to the transportation problem. It took more than average imagination to see the far greater possibilities of steam power applied to the roadway of rails.

The few who had this imagination were not always among the young and venturesome. At the laying of the cornerstone of the new railway starting from Baltimore, the aged Charles Carroll of Carrollton, then the only surviving signer of the Declaration of Independence, said, "I consider this among the most important acts of my life, second only to my signing the Declaration of Independence, if even it be second to that."

That took place more than forty years after the American Revolution. John Quincy Adams was President. Horse power was still the only power of locomotion on land which the people of America knew. Even in England, where there had been tramways for more than a century, and where locomotive development of a sort had been under way for twenty-five years, there was still the greatest skepticism as to the value of the steam locomotive. In America the first railroad to the West, that from Baltimore, was started as a double-track line for cars to be pulled by horses. Not until the new railroad from Baltimore had reached Ellicott's Mills, thirteen miles out, did a locomotive appear upon it.

That locomotive was the tiny "Tom Thumb," designed and built by Peter Cooper, a New York merchant, out of such strange materials as discarded musket barrels. The little engine was ingloriously beaten in a race with the best horse of the stage-coaching firm which furnished the regular four-footed motive power for the new railroad, but "Tom Thumb" showed that he could run.

18

The "Stevens Crampton"
Camden & Amboy R.R.
1848

THE "STEVENS CRAMPTON"

Of all the varied and diverse designs of engines tried out in the development of the American locomotive, none was stranger than this. Robert L. Stevens, president of the Camden & Amboy, got the idea in Europe, from the Crampton engine. With the aid of Isaac Dripps, his mechanical adviser, he designed an engine with a single pair of eight-foot driving wheels, intended for fast passenger service. The principal difficulties with the design were poor starting and low pulling power, which were caused by the excessively high drivers and the incorrect design of the cylinder proportions. But, if tradition be true, nothing could catch a "Stevens Crampton" once it got going.

19

In 1829, the summer of the "Tom Thumb" experiment, the Delaware and Hudson Canal Company imported an English-built locomotive, the "Stourbridge Lion," to haul coal cars on a track between its mines and its canals in Pennsylvania. It proved to be a failure—too heavy for the light track on which it was to run. Horatio Allen, who brought it from England, drove it alone on its trial run along the short stretch of hemlock-timber, iron-shod tracks. According to his own account, "the impression was very general that the iron monster would either break down the road or that it would leave the track at the curve and plunge into the creek." It returned without accident but, after further trials, was finally removed from the track and left standing by the side of the railroad. Ornamented in front with a large, fierce-looking lion in bold relief, the engine was an object of great dread to timid children, who would go out of their way to avoid passing the strange beast.

In September of that same year, 1829, the president and directors of the South Carolina Canal and Railroad Company met in the city of Charleston to decide how their line of railroad should be built—whether for horses or for steam. Before them appeared young Horatio Allen, their newly appointed chief engineer, the man who had gone to England, had brought back the "Stourbridge Lion," and had driven it on its first and last run only a few weeks before. It had not been a promising summer for locomotives in America.

"But," said bold young Allen to his directors, "there is no reason to expect any material improvement in the breed of horses, while the man is not living who knows what the breed of locomotives is to place at our command." Whereupon the farseeing directors then and there abandoned the idea of horse operation for their proposed line and, for the first time in the history of the world, undertook to build a railroad for steam locomotion only.

"The locomotive alone," they declared, "shall be used. The perfection

THE "PIONEER"

Thirty-seventh in the Baldwin line, the "Pioneer" was built in 1836 for the Utica & Schenectady Railroad. From the Mohawk Valley she was sold to the Michigan Central, where she was known as the "Alert." Sold again to a little prairie line starting westward from a village on the shore of Lake Michigan, the "Alert" traveled by lake schooner to become, in 1848, the "Pioneer" of the Galena & Chicago Union Railroad. In this way the little third-hand engine became the pioneer both of the future greatest railroad center of the world and of the Chicago & North Western Line. The "Pioneer" has been an honored feature of historical transportation exhibits.

of this power and its application to railroads is fast maturing, and will certainly reach, within the period of constructing our road, a degree of excellence which will render the application of animal power a gross abuse to the gifts and genius of science."

However, the directors of the new railroad did not quite have the courage of their conviction, for after their decision they offered a prize of $500 for the best horse-power locomotive, and in 1829 and 1830 they also tested a sail car which could sail within four points of the wind. But the result of these experiments served to strengthen their determination to tie the future of their railroad to the future of steam power.

Their first locomotive, and the first in America in regular service—the "Best Friend of Charleston"—proved itself capable of making twice the required speed of ten miles an hour. They soon had to add a second engine, known as the "West Point," which on its trial run carried 117 passengers (of whom fifty were ladies) in the four cars and nine persons on the engine, with six bales of cotton on the "barrier car." The barrier car, just back of the tender, served as a rampart between the locomotive and the passenger cars, in case of explosion or other accident.

In New York, in the summer after the South Carolina Railroad started operations, the little "DeWitt Clinton" competed successfully with horse-drawn coaches on the railway from Schenectady to Albany. Ten cars took part in the race—a train of three drawn by the locomotive and a "brigade" of seven by a single horse each. The trip was made by the locomotive in forty-six minutes and by the cars drawn by horses in about an hour and a quarter.

A Judge Gillis who happened to be in Albany when the "DeWitt Clinton" was about to make its first run stayed over a few days in order to

WINANS' "CAMELS"

Ross Winans was one of those versatile Americans of the early nineteenth century who, without training or tradition to guide them, learned how to build, equip, and operate railroads. A horse trader, he came to Baltimore to sell the new Baltimore & Ohio Railroad its four-footed motive power. He ended by building its cars; by being one of the men who developed the distinctive American practice of a swiveling truck under each end of a long car; by running the B. & O. shops; and by building for that road an unusual and interesting line of locomotives. His famous "Camels" were as ungainly in looks as the name implies, but they were successful in the 1840's in heavy freight traffic and mountain work. Henry Tyson later developed the same idea in ten-wheelers.

gratify his curiosity by "a first ride after a locomotive." Some years afterward he wrote of the experience:

"The train was composed of coach-bodies . . . placed upon trucks. The trucks were coupled together with chains . . . leaving from two to three feet slack, and when the locomotive started it took up the slack by jerks, with sufficient force to jerk the passengers, who sat on seats across the top of the coaches, out from under their hats, and in stopping they came together with such force as to send them flying from their seats. . . .

"There being no smoke or spark-catcher for the smoke-stack a volume of black smoke, strongly impregnated with sparks, coals, and cinders, came pouring back the whole length of the train. Each of the outside passengers who had an umbrella, used it as a protection against the smoke and fire. They were found to be but a momentary protection, for I think in the first mile the last one went overboard, all having their covers burnt off, when a general melee took place among the deck passengers, each whipping his neighbor to put out the fire.

"The incidents off the train were quite as striking as those on the train. . . . Everybody, together with his wife and all his children, came from a distance with all kinds of conveyances, and, being as ignorant of what was coming as their horses, drove . . . as near as they could get, only looking for the best position to get a view of the train. As it approached the horses took fright and wheeled, upsetting buggies, carriages and wagons . . . and it is not now positively known if some of them have yet stopped."

The year 1831, in the presidency of Andrew Jackson, marked the practical beginning of American steam-railroad operation. A year later locomotives were running on twenty-three miles of tracks in Maryland, South Carolina, New York, Pennsylvania, Massachusetts, and New Jersey.

The GOWAN & MARX 1839

"GOWAN & MARX"

Built in 1839 by Eastwick and Harrison of Philadelphia, the "Gowan & Marx" was one of the earliest of the great eight-wheelers which became known as the "American" type. On one of her first trips, on the Reading, she hauled 423 tons—forty times her own weight—at a speed of ten miles an hour, and at once became a sensation of the day. The reputation of American locomotives was such that when the Czar began building railroads a few years later, Eastwick and Harrison were induced to close their Philadelphia shops and go to Russia to build locomotives there. Another American who went to Russia about the same time to assist in developing railroads was a military and civil engineer, Lieutenant George Whistler, father of the artist James McNeill Whistler.

Horses continued to be used, but the new engines were improving fast. For each forty-eight-mile round trip of the Long Island Railroad, which in 1838 reached from Brooklyn as far as Hicksville, an engine burned one cord of wood, plus five-eighths of a cord to get up steam; and repair charges averaged $1.50 to $2.00 daily for each engine. This road carried freight at two and one-half cents per mile for every 100 pounds, or fifty cents per mile for every ton.

By 1840 over 1,800 miles of steam-railway tracks were finished and in operation, and in another ten years the total was nearly 9,000 miles. Railroad building was epidemic. During the forties the average annual increase of railway tracks was about 300 miles; in the fifties the annual increase was more than 2,000 miles; and by 1860 a total of 30,000 miles of track was in operation.

At the celebration of the completion of the Baltimore & Ohio Railroad to Wheeling, in 1853, an official recalled the days, only sixteen years earlier, when the chief carrier of goods and produce between Baltimore and Wheeling was a wagon company with one wagon arriving and departing each day from each terminus—a wagon carrying two and one-half tons and taking eight days for the trip. The wagon company at that time looked forward to increasing the daily arrivals and departures from one to three wagons, and eventually to five. Sixteen years later, when the railroad finally reached Wheeling, the run from Baltimore took only thirty-six hours, and 1,000 tons were being transported daily; "the weight of the tonnage-engine alone . . . almost equals the weight of the five loads that limited the hopes of the wagon company."

The War between the States increased the need while it hampered the construction of locomotives and rail lines, but by 1870 there were about 50,000 miles of track in use. An English observer in 1868 wrote that the

THE "PRESIDENT" AND THE "TIGER"

Built in 1856, these two Baldwin ten-wheelers show the trend of the day. From pilot to drawbar, locomotives were ornamented. Artists or craftsmen from other trades were called in to paint scenes on headlights, cab panels, and the like. Brasswork was applied in delicate scrolls. Cabs—unknown on the earliest engines—were marvels of hand-carved mahogany. Gold lettering in elaborate design was put on in profusion. Now that the locomotive has developed into a machine of technical beauty and harmony of design, it is no longer necessary to look for ornamentation to "gild the lily." Today's locomotive, correctly conceived, is an achievement of beauty and harmony in itself.

railway in the United States "is regarded as the pioneer of colonization and as instrumental in opening up new and fertile territories of vast extent in the West. . . . Hence, railway construction in that country was scarcely interrupted by the great Civil War; at the commencement of which Mr. Seward publicly expressed the opinion that 'physical bonds, such as highways, railroads, rivers and canals, are vastly more powerful for holding civil communities together than any mere covenants, though written on parchment or engraved on iron.' "

Two thousand miles of plains and mountains and deserts stretched between the Pacific Coast and the eastern settlements when William H. Seward spoke. Men of vision had long dreamed of a connection; men of action had already started to build from West to East, and from East to West. Under stress of war conditions the lines were driven through to meet in Utah and so, in 1869, to achieve a great continental union from the Atlantic to the Pacific.

Few persons believed, when the first line across the continent was proposed, that it would ever be finished or, if finished, that it could ever become self-supporting. Before it was finished, however, others were already projected and even under way. Since that time the whole United States, and Canada and Mexico as well, have been covered with a network of rail lines.

Even more striking than the spread of the rail net over the continent have been the evolution and improvement of the road of rails and of the locomotive engines which use it. Without the Iron Horse and the steam power that was its breath of life it might have been true, as Thomas Jefferson predicted in 1803, that it would be a thousand years before the territory west of the Mississippi would be tamed and settled.

The "JOSEPHINE"

THE "JOSEPHINE"

This early Canadian engine, imported from England in 1850, ran on the Ontario, Simcoe & Huron Railroad. True to the English design of the period, the pistons were connected to cranks on the main driving axle inside the wheels. Matched in a contest with the American-built "Lady Elgin," the "Josephine" overhauled and passed her when the American engine stopped to take on water. The incident gave quite an impetus to the use of English-built locomotives on the Canadian lines of that time.

CHAPTER II

The Power of Steam

TRACTIVE power is the measure of the ability of a locomotive to start a train; horsepower is the measure of its ability to keep a train rolling. To break out and start the first car in a train, a locomotive must exert a pull of as much as thirty pounds for each ton of the car's weight. As the cars get to rolling, one after another, the power needed to start each additional ton grows less until finally, when the whole train is started, as little as three or four pounds of tractive power per ton may be enough to keep it rolling on straight and level track. To draw a ton of weight up a grade rising one foot in a hundred —that is, a grade of one per cent—requires an additional twenty pounds of tractive effort; to pull it around curves requires, figuring roughly, about one pound of tractive effort for each degree of curvature in the track.

For operating purposes railroads are divided into divisions; and those are subdivided into engine districts, usually about 100 miles in length. The locomotives of the railroad are classified by their size, power, wheel arrangement, and other characteristics. Each class of engine, whether freight or passenger, large or small, has a "tonnage rating" for each district over which it operates. To determine how heavy a train each class of engine can pull over a given

30

THE "GENERAL"

Central figure in the greatest of all railroad loco-motive races, the "General" now stands in honored retirement at Chattanooga. During the War between the States, at a critical time when the Southern armies depended on the line of railroad between Atlanta and Chattanooga for supplies, James J. Andrews and twenty-one other Union soldiers penetrated the Confederate lines in dis-guise, seized the "General" at Big Shanty, Georgia, cut it loose from its train, and raced northward, intending to burn bridges, destroy track, and put the line out of commission. W. A. Fuller and other Confederates, pursuing on foot, on handcar, and on three other engines, in succession, kept so closely behind Andrews that he was unable to carry out his plans and finally was overhauled and captured.

31

district, however, other things must be considered besides the power of the locomotive and the grades to be climbed and curves to be rounded. A train weighing 5,000 tons, concentrated in fifty heavily loaded cars, for example,

TO BREAK OUT AND START

THE FIRST CAR THE LOCOMOTIVE MUST EXERT A PULL OF 30 POUNDS PER TON

can be pulled with less power than a train of the same total weight but made up of a larger number of more lightly loaded cars.

The tractive effort of the locomotive depends upon the weight resting on

AS EACH SUCCEEDING CAR IS STARTED, THE PULL REQUIRED IS LESS AND LESS

UNTIL ONLY A FEW POUNDS PER TON IS REQUIRED TO KEEP THE TRAIN IN MOTION ON A LEVEL TRACK

its driving wheels; upon its steam pressure in pounds per square inch; upon the size of the cylinders in which this pressure is used; and upon the diameter of the driving wheels. For any given weight of locomotive, the higher the steam pressure, the larger the cylinders, and the smaller the driving wheels, the greater

TO PULL A TRAIN UP A 1 PER CENT GRADE

THE LOCOMOTIVE MUST EXERT AN ADDITIONAL PULL OF 20 POUNDS PER TON

is the starting power. But speed calls for large driving wheels, so that sustained speed with heavy loads, particularly on grades, demands not only high drivers

32

THE "MOGUL"

The "Mogul" got its name from the popular impression given by the mighty pullers of freight which appeared in the late 1860's and by 1875 were replacing the eight-wheeled "Americans" on an increasing number of freight trains. The "Mogul" had the same number of wheels as the "American," but six of the wheels instead of four were drivers. This increase in the proportion of their weight on drivers gave them distinctly more power than the double-purpose "American." Of all locomotive names "Mogul" is the one best known. The true "Mogul" was a 2-6-0—two leading wheels, six drivers coupled, no trailing wheels. The type itself is practically extinct, but the name goes on forever. To the uninitiated, "Mogul" means any big engine, passenger or freight.

but high steam pressure, large cylinders, and great capacity in the boiler to keep up the supply of steam, mile after mile.

It is in its great horsepower at high speed that the modern steam locomotive most excels its predecessors of even a few years ago. The average

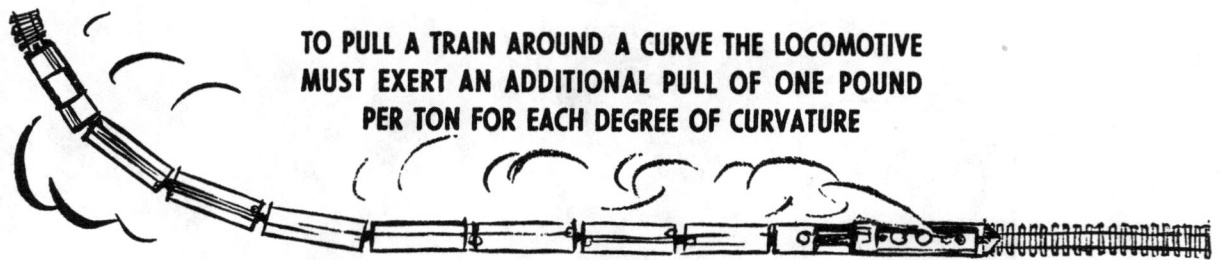

TO PULL A TRAIN AROUND A CURVE THE LOCOMOTIVE
MUST EXERT AN ADDITIONAL PULL OF ONE POUND
PER TON FOR EACH DEGREE OF CURVATURE

tractive effort of all locomotives in service ten years ago was about 38,000 pounds—enough to handle on straight, level track a freight train weighing about 4,500 tons, of about 100 loaded box cars. The average tractive effort of all locomotives in service now is about 48,000 pounds—enough to handle a train of about 5,500 tons under the same conditions. The more striking differ-

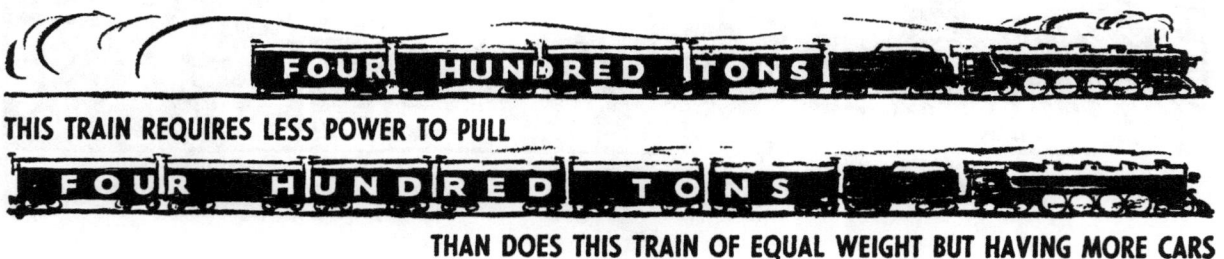

FOUR HUNDRED TONS

THIS TRAIN REQUIRES LESS POWER TO PULL

FOUR HUNDRED TONS

THAN DOES THIS TRAIN OF EQUAL WEIGHT BUT HAVING MORE CARS

ence, though, is in the behavior of the two engines at speeds of forty miles an hour and more. Here the modern engine, with its greater steaming capacity, will develop sustained horsepower twice that of the older engines. It pulls heavier loads, pulls them faster, and keeps up its performance longer.

In developing the steam locomotive as the prime mover of the commerce of the American continent, almost every possible combination of size and

34

THE "CONSOLIDATION"

When the Lehigh Valley Railroad was formed by the consolidation of a number of smaller lines, it ordered new engines. Alexander Mitchell designed them in 1866, with two leading wheels, eight drivers coupled, no trailing wheels. Born with the consolidation of the Lehigh Valley, the type became known as the "Consolidation." These models were, for more than twenty years, the standard for freight locomotives, the backbone of railroad power. From them, in lineal descent, sprang the line of modern heavy freight locomotives. America owes much to the 2-8-0 locomotive which conquered grades, cut costs, and handled the growing commerce of a continent as no previous means of transportation possibly could have done. Many a good "Consolidation" is still in service, usually in branch-line work.

arrangement of boiler, cylinders, and wheels has been used. Emphasis on the different elements of the design of locomotives has varied with varying needs. New ways have been tried; some have been adopted, many discarded. But the net result has been steady progress in moving heavier loads and moving them faster—in doing more and more actual transportation work.

In railroad language a "ton-mile" is a unit measure of work, representing a ton hauled one mile. In the years just after the World War the average freight train in the United States produced less than 7,500 ton-miles for each hour it was on the road. Today's trains not only are heavier but move at an average speed nearly half again higher than those of fifteen years ago, so that they produce an average of nearly 12,000 ton-miles of transportation an hour. This figure is an average for all locomotives and all trains on all lines in the United States. Large engines pulling full loads under favorable circumstances accomplish far more, of course.

Remarkable results of this sort were not attained all at once. From the very beginning there were stubborn problems to be solved in the production and use of steam. The solution of one problem frequently raised others—and still does. Most of these problems are not the sort which can be answered by theory only, or even in the laboratory. They can be answered finally and satisfactorily only by actual trial under conditions of railroad operation.

The earliest of all problems for the locomotive designer was that of steam pressure. The power of an engine to do work depends upon the difference between the pressure in the boiler and the pressure in the place into which the steam is discharged or exhausted. The stationary engines of James Watt used steam at pressure little higher than the fifteen pounds per square inch of the atmosphere. To make the steam do work, it had to be exhausted from the engine cylinder into the partial vacuum of a condenser. But condensers were

"JANUS"

William Mason, master builder of Taunton, Massachusetts, designed the facing-both-ways "Janus" for the Lehigh Valley Railroad in 1871. It was intended for heavy duty on mountain grades. The germ of the same idea, two engines built together under the control of one engineer, may be found in the "South Carolina," the double-ender which Horatio Allen had designed nearly forty years before. Its development is seen in the Fairlie double-enders which negotiated the grades climbing the mountain between Veracruz and Mexico City before the Mexican Railway was electrified. An offshoot of the same principle is seen in the many articulated "Mallet" engines in use today.

too large, heavy, and cumbersome for locomotive engines at that time. If locomotives were to work, their steam had to be raised to a pressure well above that of the atmosphere—a pressure which seemed dangerously high to Watt and the early builders of low-pressure steam engines.

TRACTIVE EFFORT OF A LOCOMOTIVE DEPENDS UPON VARIATION IN

IN POUNDS PER SQUARE INCH

1. STEAM PRESSURE   **2. SIZE OF CYLINDER**   **3. DIAMETER OF DRIVING WHEELS**

The venturesome and ingenious Trevithick, in 1803, got the steam pressure needed for the first high-pressure locomotive engine to run on tracks by forcing the draft of the fire. This he did, not with any complicated arrangement of bellows or blowers, but by turning the exhaust steam from the cylinders right up the smokestack into the open air—just as the draft on loco-

NEITHER OF THESE TWO LOCOMOTIVES CAN MOVE THE OTHER, FOR THEY ARE EXACTLY ALIKE

motives is forced today. Ten years later William Hedley proved the theory of adhesion—that the weight of the locomotive was enough to enable smooth driving wheels to pull on smooth rails without slipping. Fifteen years after Hedley's demonstration George Stephenson combined the known elements of design, with certain major improvements of his own, into his famous locomotive, the "Rocket."

38

STEAM ON THE "L"

On the elevated railroads of cities, steam power long ago yielded to electric, but the steam-powered "dummy" cars which once served as surface transportation are faintly remembered, thanks to the ancient ballad, "On the Dummy Line." But when steam began to supplant horse power for city transportation, the name of Mathias N. Forney was known in the land—and still is, among locomotive students—for Forney not only designed the locomotive type which bears his name but edited the *Railroad Gazette* for many years. The locomotive, he thought, should be separate from the car it propelled, so that it might be used first with one car and then another, "just as one horse may pull any vehicle." In urban service his locomotives rapidly replaced the self-propelled unit car of that day.

THE HIGH-PRESSURE
LOCOMOTIVE   *can pull*   THE LOW-PRESSURE
LOCOMOTIVE

These early steps in locomotive development took place in England. The
next great step in the use of steam was taken in the United States. The
"Rocket" carried a steam pressure of fifty pounds to the square inch. It could
not carry more because the joints in the pipes, through which the steam must

THE LOCOMOTIVE WITH
LARGER CYLINDERS   *can pull*   THE LOCOMOTIVE WITH
SMALLER CYLINDERS

pass, were merely heavy canvas coated with red lead. Within five years Baldwin,
the American watchmaker who turned locomotive builder, had developed a
steam-tight metal joint which would carry double the pressure of the British
joints. Pressures increased gradually until, about the time of the World War,
pressures of 200 pounds per square inch were usual. Today, 250 pounds is

THE LOCOMOTIVE WITH
LARGER DRIVE WHEELS   *can run
away from*   THE LOCOMOTIVE WITH
SMALLER DRIVE WHEELS

40

A HIGH-SPEED TEN-WHEELER

As trains grew in size and weight, the old 4-4-0 "American" type gave way to the ten-wheeler 4-6-0, designed and used for both passenger and freight service. Long after it was displaced in freight service by the "Mogul" and the "Consoli-dation," the ten-wheeler continued to pull most of the heavier passenger trains until the turn of the century. The one here pictured hauled the original "Royal Blue" train between Washington and Jersey City.

the normal standard, with many locomotives carrying much higher pressures. To develop such high pressures, however, requires far more than merely steam-tight metal joints. It requires metals which combine the necessary lightness with great strength—such metals as the metallurgists have been developing ever since the introduction of steel on a commercial scale, and especially during the past few years. It requires strong fireboxes to withstand the pressure, and big fireboxes with ample surfaces where the direct heat of the flames may be transmitted to the water. To keep up the supply of steam requires ample boiler capacity; to keep the steam hot and dry and "live" requires efficient superheaters—an arrangement by which the steam passes through small tubes looped in the flues where the hot gases rush from the fire to the smokestack. In such tubes the temperature of the steam may be raised to 750° Fahrenheit.

Long before locomotives or even stationary steam engines were in use, it had been found that steam shut up without a way of escape would burst the vessel in which it was confined. It was not difficult to devise a valve which would let excess steam escape. The difficulty lay in making an automatic valve which would open promptly when the pressure inside the boiler went beyond the proper point, and would close promptly as soon as the pressure was reduced a few pounds below that point. Early locomotive safety valves would open all right but, once open, they might let half the steam in the boiler get away before they closed themselves. The fireman of the "Best Friend of Charleston" who caused the first locomotive-boiler explosion by holding down his safety valve may have done it because he was tired of losing fifteen or twenty pounds of the steam, which he had worked to build up, every time the safety valve opened.

That particular problem of a satisfactory safety valve was not solved until 1866, when George W. Richardson of the Troy & Boston invented the

THE "COLUMBIA"

Developed in 1892, the four-hundredth anniversary of Columbus' discovery of America, this 2-4-2 type of the Baldwin Works was named the "Columbia." The purpose of the trailing axle was to support a firebox of greater area than was possible in the "American," then the standard passenger type. The "Columbia" type was never widely used in the country of its birth, because of the prejudice at that time against running engines at high speed with only one pair of leading wheels rather than with a four-wheel leading truck. In England, France, and Russia, however, engines of the "Columbia" type successfully hauled light express trains for many years.

valve which pops open at the pressure for which it is set and closes itself smartly when the pressure falls a pound or two below that point. The "pop"

THE EARLY SAFETY VALVE

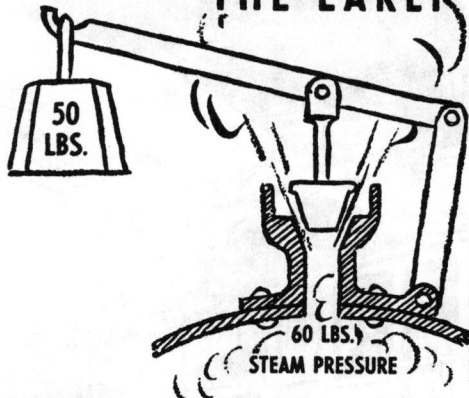

WHEN THE STEAM PRESSURE BECAME GREATER THAN THE WEIGHT, THE VALVE LIFTED AND STEAM ESCAPED

WHEN THE FIREMAN OF THE "BEST FRIEND" HELD DOWN THIS VALVE, STEAM PRESSURE INCREASED UNTIL THE BOILER BURST

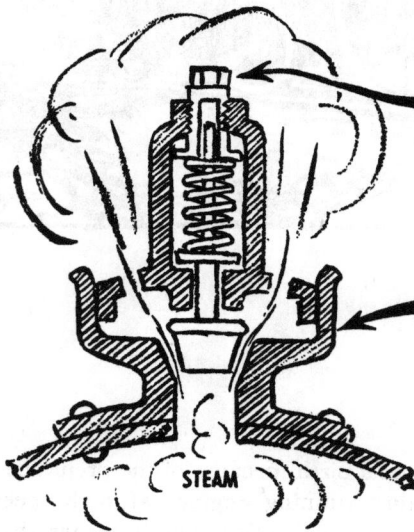

SCREW FOR ADJUSTING TENSION ON SPRING. THIS DETERMINES EXACTLY WHAT PRESSURE WILL FORCE VALVE OPEN. SPRING WILL CLOSE VALVE WHEN PRESSURE DROPS

"Pop" valve

with which it opens not only has given the name "pop valve" to the device for the release of excess steam but has added to railroad language the phrase

THE "999"

She needs no name other than "999"—for no locomotive is more famous than the New York Central's eight-wheeler which, in May, 1893, pulled the "Empire State Express" over a measured mile at 112.5 miles an hour—the first time in history that any vehicle built and driven by man had gone faster than 100 miles an hour. The man who drove the "999," Engineer Charlie Hogan, became the idol of speed fans; and the locomotive became a museum piece, carefully preserved at the West Albany shops of the railroad, whence it still is carried to great expositions and transportation shows.

"popping off," applied not only to locomotives but to the man who relieves the pressure of his feelings by the employment of explosive language.

But making steam and keeping it in the boiler until needed are only the beginning. Other valves and valve gear control the admission of the steam into the cylinders, and its exhaust from them, in such fashion as to cause the wheels of the engine to turn forward or backward, fast or slow, and to do it without undue loss of power. Control of steam to make it do the work desired has been one of the more difficult problems in locomotive development. A throttle to let the steam pass from boiler to cylinders was not difficult to devise, but here again the development of valves to time and control the movement has been the subject of vast study, discussion, and experiment.

To start a train calls for all of the engine's power. The cylinders need a full charge of steam through the full stroke of the pistons. Then, as the train picks up speed, the engineer may conserve steam by running with valves set so as to cut off the supply early in the stroke, letting the expansive power of the steam push the pistons on to the end. By proper adjustment of the valves which cut off the steam entering the cylinders, speed may be maintained with relatively small consumption of steam and fuel.

With the mastery of the mechanical problems which confronted the early builders, the American steam locomotive has grown into today's machine of grace and power—a machine which does not even look like the Iron Horse of other days.

Other forms of locomotive power have recently been added to steam power—smooth, silent electric engines, drawing their power through wires from great central power stations; humming Diesels, burning oil fuel inside their cylinders and driving their wheels through electric motors—each kind of locomotive having its own place in the job of moving men and their goods.

VAUCLAIN'S COMPOUND

Probably the most successful—certainly the most famous—of compound engines built for high speed were those designed by Samuel M. Vauclain, famous locomotive master of Baldwin's. Forty years ago this Atlantic-type "Vauclain" compound hauled the express between Camden and Atlantic City, day after day, at an average speed of 71 miles an hour, with bursts of speed as high as 110 or even 115 miles an hour. At such speeds, even with her high drivers, pistons in each of the four cylinders had to travel back and forth five times in each second. That meant that each piston started from rest, got up a speed of more than thirty feet a second, and came back to rest—all within one-tenth of a second. The use of compound locomotives has greatly declined in late years.

CHAPTER III

Wheels and More Wheels

As FAR back as 1812 Colonel John Stevens of Hoboken published his *Documents Tending To Prove the Superiority of Rail-Ways and Steam-Carriages over Canal Navigation*. This was nine years after Trevithick's engine was built, but seventeen years before the "Tom Thumb" and the "Stourbridge Lion" were tried out on American railroads. The colonel was ahead of his time. Nowhere was there in operation a "rail-way and steam-carriage" such as he described.

The United States through the 1820's and the 1830's, like Europe, went in for canal building. But by 1840 it had become apparent that the Iron Horse, puffing along on tracks, was to be the answer to the great need for transportation. The creature had shown its ability to do the work. It had begun to be accepted as part of the American way of doing things. Even the cattle in the pastures, which had scampered away in fright from the first fire-breathing monsters, had come to accept their daily passing as a matter of course, calling for no more than a brief glance up from their contented grazing. Horses no longer had to be held at the head when the trains went by, and people had formed the habit, in those towns so fortunate as to have railroads, of going down to the depot to see the trains come in.

48

A "JOINTED" ENGINE

Anatole Mallet, in France, devised a locomotive which was really two engines under one long boiler, the boiler supplying steam to both sets of cylinders. The engines swiveled under the boiler, so that the whole great length of the machine could round curves. The first American "Mallet," an 0-6-6-0 in wheel arrangement, was built in 1904. Most of the early "Mallets" were compounds, using the same steam twice—expanding it in high-pressure cylinders from which it was exhausted into larger low-pressure cylinders to start work again. Greater steaming capacity has made it possible to build super-"Mallets" which make enough steam to allow its use only once at high pressure in all cylinders—thereby getting more power, higher speed, and greater simplicity.

The railroads were still short local lines, scattered about in the Atlantic seaboard states from New England to Georgia, and in the Mississippi Valley from Louisiana to Michigan. Construction was of all sorts. The distance between rails ranged from three to six feet—nearly half a century more was to pass before uniformity was to be established in gauge of track. But already, by 1840, there had emerged from the work of the early builders a distinctive American type of locomotive. Under the Whyte system of classifying locomotives by the arrangement of their wheels from front to rear, this American type was a 4-4-0—that is, an engine with four small leading wheels in a swivel truck supporting its front end; four driving wheels behind them under the boiler and firebox; no wheels behind the drivers.

This systematic designation of types of locomotives by their wheel arrangement was to come later, however. In the generation in which the 4-4-0 was almost universal in the United States the usual classification was by the shape of the smokestack—"balloon," "diamond," or "straight." The bulging balloon and the diamond-top stacks were not added to locomotives for ornament. They were spark and cinder catchers. As the use of wood for fuel passed out, the slender straight stack replaced the balloon and diamond, while the growth of the locomotive in size caused more and more of the stack to disappear from view. Today's large engines show only a short snout of a stack, but the stack is there just the same, down inside the smoke box.

Improved in certain ways, the "American" remained for thirty years the standard engine in the United States, equal to the work put upon it and not too heavy for the track and bridges upon which it ran. With the improvement of tracks, the substitution of steel for iron, and the constantly growing demand for cheaper transportation, the time came for a more powerful engine.

The "ten-wheeler," a 4-6-0, with three pairs of drivers coupled instead

POWERFUL PUSHERS

Among the earliest "Mallets" built in America were the heavy pushers put into service by the Erie in 1907 to help freight trains over the grade out of Suffern, New York. The pusher is shown wide open, taking as much load as she can off the "front end." The compound "Mallet" type, never well adapted for fast road freight service, found a great field of usefulness in pusher work, where its great power could be brought into play at low speeds. Most of the "Mallets" built in late years are not compounds and are designed for much faster service than the early examples—in keeping with the speeding-up of freight service. The simple "Mallet," finished in 1936 for the Norfolk and Western, develops 6,500 boiler horsepower and can pull trains at seventy miles an hour.

of two, was the first successful answer to the demand. The "ten-wheeler," like the "American," was a dual-purpose engine, combining speed for passenger service and power for freight. In freight service it was followed by the "Mogul," a 2-6-0, its front end carried on one swinging axle with small leading wheels, and with three pairs of driving wheels coupled. So powerfully did the "Mogul" impress itself on the imagination and speech of its time that to this day any large locomotive is often called a "Mogul."

Close on the heels of the "Mogul" came the "Consolidation." Both were developed in the sixties to meet the increased military and commercial demands. The "Consolidation," a 2-8-0—one pair of leading wheels and four pairs of driving wheels coupled—became the standard heavy freight engine of America for a generation.

During the years in which the "Mogul" and the "Consolidation" were the standard freight locomotives, passenger trains were pulled by eight- and ten-wheelers. Before the end of the nineteenth century eight-wheel "Americans" with high driving wheels had more than once run faster than 100 miles an hour in short bursts of speed.

To pull larger, heavier trains and to pull them faster, engines needed to have larger fireboxes. But the fireboxes, carried between the rear pair of driving wheels, were necessarily narrow and of limited capacity. Various arrangements to enlarge them were tried. Some fireboxes were made wider than the frames of the engine and were built above them. The Wooten firebox, designed especially to burn anthracite, was so wide that two fire doors were provided so that the fireman could throw his coal to all parts of the grate. To get this width, the firebox was built entirely above the driving wheels.

Early in the nineties, however, there emerged a new and better balanced design—a wide firebox, deep enough for bituminous coal, projecting behind

GEARED FOR POWER

Most steam locomotives drive directly, without transmission or reduction gears—no small matter in the simplicity of the steam locomotive. The "Shay" engines, however—built for use on lumber roads and the like, where heavy hauling must be done on rough track and over difficult grades—increase their power by driving a shaft not unlike that of a steamship, which through an arrangement of cogs is geared to every axle, including those on the tender. The engine has three vertical cylinders, mounted on one side of the boiler—an arrangement which makes it necessary to have the boiler off the center line of the engine. Altogether an odd-looking affair—not fast, but with the ability to get a firm grip on the track and pull a heavy load for its size on stiff grades.

the driving wheels, and supported by an extra axle with small wheels. With the addition of this pair of trailing wheels, the "American" 4-4-0 locomotive grew into the "Atlantic" or 4-4-2; the ten-wheeler 4-6-0 grew into the "Pacific" or 4-6-2 type. The "Atlantic" became standard for light, fast passenger service, and the "Pacific" for heavy passenger service.

To meet the need for higher speeds in freight service there was a like development of the freight locomotive. A trailing axle added to the "Mogul" 2-6-0 created the "Prairie" 2-6-2—a type which did not survive in large numbers. The same addition to the "Consolidation" 2-8-0, however, created the "Mikado" 2-8-2, which early in this century became the standard locomotive for fast freight service and so remained until the World War.

By that time the next step in development had been taken in both passenger and freight service. With larger steam capacity it became possible to increase tractive power by the addition of more driving wheels. Adding a fourth pair of drivers to the "Pacific" created the 4-8-2, or "Mountain" type of passenger engine. Adding a fifth pair to the "Mikado" made the 2-10-2, or "Santa Fe" type of freight hauler.

Meanwhile, certain work required locomotives of great tractive power, without requiring sustained high speed. Accordingly there were developed such types as the "Mastodon," a 4-8-0, and the "Decapod," a 2-10-0, both with relatively small driving wheels. Later, in the 1890's, there was introduced into the United States from France the articulated compound "Mallet" type of locomotive. An articulated locomotive is really two separate engines working under one long, flexibly mounted boiler. In the compound engine the steam works twice, being exhausted from the high-pressure cylinders into low-pressure cylinders before escaping up the stack. The early "Mallets" combined articulation and compounding in a unit of great power but rather low speed.

54

HEAVY—AND FAST, TOO

The success of the 2-8-2 "Mikados," so called because first built for the Japanese railways, led to the development of the 2-10-2, known as the "Santa Fe" type because they were first built for that road. Their ten driving wheels, coupled, gave them the starting and pulling power of the "Decapods"; their large fireboxes, carried on a trailing axle, gave them the sustained steaming power and speed of the "Mikados." They remained the best examples of locomotives for heavy-duty, high-speed freight service until the development, in the late 1920's, of the type of high-horsepower engine with high drive wheels which combined the power necessary for heavy freight service with passenger-train speed. To them is partly due the 50 per cent increase in freight-train speeds in recent years.

55

The first "Mallet" in the United States was an 0-6-6-0—no leading wheels, six driving wheels coupled in the front engine, six more in the rear engine, and no axle under the firebox. By the time of the World War, "Mallet" compounds had been expanded to 2-8-8-2's and even to 2-10-10-2's.

To the inventive minds of railroad operators and locomotive designers, trailing axles supporting fireboxes and carrying weight offered another opportunity. These small low wheels could not be coupled directly with the large driving wheels, but their added adhesion could be used to get more power by means of an auxiliary booster engine geared to the axle. The booster engine is used only at starting or in pulling heavy grades at low speed, and its power is automatically cut out as the train picks up speed. A still later development of the same principle makes use of the weight of the tender to increase starting or low-speed power by means of an auxiliary engine under the tender, driving the wheels of the tender truck.

While road engines were developing along these varied lines, there were growth and change in yard or switching engines as well. In ordinary switch service the engine needs tractive power to start loads many times every day. It does not require high sustained speed nor does it need leading wheels or a guiding truck to insure steadiness at high speed. The work to be done by the switcher dictated its form—the 0-4-0, the 0-6-0, and the 0-8-0 types without leading or trailing wheels, all weight concentrated on small driving wheels to give great tractive power for starting.

Thus the American locomotive picture at the time of the World War included "Mountains" and "Pacifics" in heavy passenger service; "Atlantics," ten-wheelers, and "Americans" in light passenger service; "Santa Fe's" and "Mikados" in fast freight service; and "Mallet" compounds, "Decapods," and "Consolidations" in drag or slow freight service.

56

THE PENNSYLVANIA "PACIFICS"

One of the most remarkably successful designs for its purpose in the long history of locomotives is the "K-4" design of the Pennsylvania, developed in 1914. The "K-4," a "Pacific" type, had to be built to fit the limitations of clearances, overhead and side, and the permitted length of rigid wheel base.

The design is a triumph of speed, power, and efficiency within the limits imposed. There are larger locomotives, but today, more than twenty years after the first "K-4's" were built, engines of this type are hauling some of the world's fastest trains on the Pennsylvania.

57

CHAPTER IV

The "Breed" of Locomotives Changes

DURING the years since the World War the "breed" of locomotives in America has changed in more ways and improved more greatly than in any like period, with the possible exception of the two decades just after the year in which Horatio Allen persuaded the directors of the South Carolina Railroad to put their faith in the Iron Horse and build their railroad for steam.

Today's steam locomotive is a marvelous traveling power plant—compact, reliable, flexible, and efficient. Stationary plants get more power out of each pound of fuel burned, it is true, but the stationary plant does not have to operate within the severe limits under which the locomotive must do its work. Locomotives cannot be higher than about seventeen feet above the rail, or wider than twelve feet, because they must pass through tunnels and bridges; nor can they be more than about seventy feet long, because they must run around curves. They cannot weigh more than about 70,000 pounds per axle, because of the limits of strength of the track and bridges over which they operate. Within these severe limitations locomotive designers have created power plants which can produce and deliver more than 5,000 horsepower on demand, according to the great and sudden variations in the work to be done

THE "MOUNTAIN" TYPE

The "Mountain" type of locomotive was developed to meet a need for a locomotive with enough power to pull a heavy freight train and enough speed to pull a fast passenger train. First used by the Chesapeake and Ohio in the Mountain State of West Virginia, the type soon found wide favor as passenger trains grew in size and freight trains demanded more and more speed. The locomotive pictured is a "Mountain" type used on the Texas and Pacific, in service in west Texas between Fort Worth and El Paso. This particular class of engine is distinguished not only by great power for the purpose for which it is used but also by the most melodious, deep-toned, and pleasing whistle in the country.

in starting trains, forward or backward, and in keeping them rolling uphill and down, on straight track or around curves.

The stationary plant, not being subject to such severe and fluctuating limits and demands, is built to burn fuel more slowly and completely; to use the steam produced in turbines which turn always in the same direction and at about the same speed; and to exhaust the steam from those turbines into the partial vacuum of condensers, where the pressure may be as low as one or two pounds to the square inch, instead of exhausting it into the open air, with its pressure of fifteen pounds or more.

The rugged locomotive overcomes its disadvantages to a large extent by intensifying and speeding up the processes of combustion and the use of steam. In the furnace of a modern locomotive, combustion goes on in a perfect tempest. For each pound of fuel burned, fifty pounds of air are sucked into and through the fire. The hot gases resulting from combustion rush over and around the barrier of the fire arch and into the boiler tubes at speeds as high as 150 miles an hour.

The steam locomotive, despite its theoretically low efficiency in converting fuel into power as compared with large stationary power plants, holds its own as a unit of high over-all economic efficiency, whether measured by its output of power per cubic foot of space, or per pound of weight, or per dollar of cost.

Fifty years ago, when electric traction first appeared, predictions were often made that the steam locomotive was doomed, just as predictions are sometimes made today that it is to be supplanted by internal-combustion power. But these earlier predictions were in error. Electric traction does play its necessary part in wonderful railroad developments. On the Milwaukee Road, the Great Northern, the Virginian, the Norfolk and Western, the Boston and Maine, the New Haven, the New York Central, the Lackawanna, the Reading,

60

A MODERN COMPOUND

No locomotive designer of ancient or modern times has been more daring and progressive than John E. Muhlfeld. This heavy-duty compound designed by him for the Delaware and Hudson, and built by the American Locomotive Company in 1930, is the heaviest and most powerful consolidation type ever constructed. It is one of four locomotives of distinctive design built for the Delaware and Hudson in recent years. All have water-tube high-pressure boilers, making steam at from 350 to 500 pounds pressure per square inch, and developing great fuel efficiency and great pulling power in freight service. The latest of the four, the "L. F. Loree," uses the same steam three times by triple expansion in its four cylinders—one high pressure, one intermediate, and two low pressure.

the Illinois Central, the Pennsylvania, and the Baltimore & Ohio—in Canada and in Mexico—electric traction has been used with great success to meet special conditions. Steam, however, continues to be the mainstay for power in the general run of American railroad operation.

One reason for this is the capacity for change and development which the steam locomotive has shown throughout its history, and particularly in the past ten or twenty years. Ten years ago few steam locomotives could develop more than 4,500 horsepower. Today, 5,000 to 6,000 horsepower is not unusual, and there is in operation, on the Norfolk and Western Railway, a "Mallet" locomotive of 6,500 horsepower, which can make seventy miles an hour pulling a heavy-tonnage freight train. The modern locomotive not only can do more work per pound of weight than the locomotive of earlier days but can do it on less fuel per pound of work done. On the average performance of all locomotives in service in the United States, two ounces of coal, turning half a pint of water into steam, will make enough power to haul a ton a mile. That is not high compared to the theoretical power of the heat in two ounces of coal, but it is high as an average of practical performance in turning heat into power and power into work.

Under the hands of the engineer and fireman of a modern locomotive are levers and handles which can start, stop, and control not only the 200 or 300 tons of traveling power plant in whose cab they ride but the thousands of tons of loaded cars trailing behind. The cab itself is hardly to be recognized as the descendant of the painted and gilded cabs of the early years.

Today's cab has the same essential controls, but grown and changed almost beyond recognition. There are ingenious throttles, designed to let enough steam enter the cylinders when engines are "drifting" downhill to keep them from getting dry. A separate throttle controls the cutting-in of the

62

THE "HANDSOME HUDSONS"

"Handsome is as handsome does" holds quite true for the "Hudson," a 4-6-4 type developed by the New York Central ten years ago. The "Hudson" has shown its power and stamina by hauling the fastest trains all the way from Harmon, New York, to Chicago. At Harmon the electric operation of the New York Central ends. Developed to meet a need for great speed and power combined, the "Hudson" is a harmonious design, of rare grace and balance as well as of great power. Since the day it was born, this type has been a beloved subject of "engine picture fans" and locomotive model makers.

booster engine, if the locomotive has one. The familiar long-necked oilcan of the engineer has given way to automatic lubrication in many parts of the locomotive. The reverse lever, on large engines, is operated by the power of compressed air. The engine brake lever has been replaced, for the entire train, by the controls of the air-brake system. The whistle may be blown and the bell rung automatically by compressed air. The water pump has given way to the injector, which puts water into the boiler whether the engine is running or standing. The hand-opened fire door has been replaced, on most engines, with automatic doors which open at the pressure of a foot on a treadle. On large engines the fireman, instead of throwing coal himself with a scoop, operates an automatic stoker which brings coal forward from the tender on an inclosed screw conveyor, lifts it, and sprays it over the surface of the fire. On oil-burning engines, of course, there is no coal to be thrown. The engineer and fireman, in short, have become the operators of a complete, compact, and efficient power plant on wheels.

Throughout the development of the locomotive there has been constant experiment in adjusting the proportions of the firebox and the boiler, where the steam is made, and the cylinders in which it does its work. It is not recorded that any locomotive was ever like the little steamboat with the big whistle which used so much steam that the boat had to stop every time the whistle was blown. Ambitious designers, however, who sought to increase the power of their locomotives by simply enlarging the size of the cylinders soon found that while such engines might start well, they couldn't keep running without boilers big enough to meet the demand of the cylinders for steam.

Bigger boilers called for larger and more efficient fireboxes. So we have heavy-duty, high-speed locomotives built since the World War, with long, wide fireboxes supported on the two axles of a four-wheel trailing truck. In their

THE WORLD'S LARGEST

These Northern Pacific 2-8-8-4 "Mallets" are the largest and most powerful steam locomotives now in use. The locomotive itself weighs 715,000 pounds. With the tender the whole great machine weighs 1,116,000 pounds. It has four cylinders, each twenty-six by thirty-two inches, working steam "simple" at 250 pounds pressure. With sixty-three-inch driving wheels the locomotive has a tractive force of 139,000 pounds, which can be increased, by the use of the booster engine at starting or on heavy grades, to 153,300 pounds. Its firebox, with a grate area of 182 square feet, is big enough to hold ten persons seated around a dinner table. Such a locomotive has power enough to haul a 17,000-ton train on level track—more, of course, than would be pulled in ordinary service.

furnaces there are brick arches to keep the flames in the furnace longer, and siphons to circulate the water where the fire is hottest. On many engines the water is preheated with steam from the exhaust before it goes into the boiler.

In the manner of using the steam there is another change that does not meet the casual eye. Forty years ago there was a great movement toward compound locomotives, that is, engines with more than one pair of cylinders, in which the steam was worked twice by exhausting it from high-pressure to low-pressure cylinders before letting it escape into the atmosphere. Such engines had the advantage of higher fuel efficiency; but they had the disadvantage of complications and of relatively low power, particularly in starting. Twenty years ago most "Mallets" and other locomotives with two pairs of cylinders were compounds. With the improvement in steaming capacity in recent years, especially with the use of superheaters for steam, there has been a striking development of the simple "Mallet" type—that is, working with all four cylinders using high-pressure steam drawn direct from the boiler and exhausted into the open air. Such locomotives must have great capacity to produce steam, but they can draw at high sustained speed heavy trains such as were considered possible only in drag freight service just a few years ago.

The addition of the four-wheel trailing truck to carry larger fireboxes created a whole new line of wheel arrangements and engine types. The "Pacific" 4-6-2 passenger engine grew into the "Hudson" 4-6-4; the "Mountain" 4-8-2 grew into the 4-8-4. In freight service the "Mikado" 2-8-2 became the "Berkshire" 2-8-4; the "Santa Fe" 2-10-2 grew into the "Texas" 2-10-4. New types of still different wheel arrangements were developed, such as the "Union Pacific" 4-12-2 with twelve driving wheels coupled—the largest non-articulated design in use. The new "Mallets" also often have four-wheel trailing trucks rather than single trailing axles.

66

PULLING—NOT PUSHING

This Southern Pacific "Mallet" is pulling a train through the Sierra Nevada, not pushing the train as it might seem to be doing at a hasty glance. To get the engine crew forward, where the view is better and where the crew is in front of hot gases from the engine blast in snowsheds and tunnels, the usual arrangement of parts is reversed. The cab is over the front truck; the firebox is at the front end of the boiler, and the smokestack is at the rear; the tender is next behind the smokestack. Such an arrangement is possible only with oil fuel, which is brought forward the length of the engine in pipes. The arrangement is logical and successful in meeting the conditions, but startling to see, nevertheless.

67

Most of today's newer giant locomotives rest on one-piece cast-steel beds which carry the whole great mechanism securely, without twist or strain. Such frames, with their great strength and rigidity, help to reduce the work required to maintain modern locomotives in good order, and so increase their economy and reliability in service.

The cast-steel engine bed, however, is only one factor in the development of more continuous service and longer runs as part of the regular life of the steam locomotive. The old idea that the engine had to go into the roundhouse after running 100 or 150 miles to have its fire dropped and to receive a thorough going-over has been discarded within the past few years. Extended runs, covering two or more engine districts, are no longer unusual. Steam locomotives are regularly making continuous runs, for example, between Kansas City and Birmingham, and between Los Angeles and El Paso.

Continuous runs overnight between Denver and Chicago have been made by the Burlington's "Aeolus," a steam locomotive streamlined in a sheathing of stainless steel, used upon occasion to relieve the regular Diesel locomotives on the "Zephyr" trains. The reciprocating parts of the "Aeolus"—pistons, rods, and other moving parts which work back-and-forth and up-and-down to transmit the power of steam to the wheels—are of light alloys of steel and aluminum. These parts, in the conventional locomotive of equal power, weigh more than a ton on each side of the engine. On the "Aeolus" this weight has been reduced to less than a thousand pounds to a side, with corresponding saving in the stresses set up on the track and in the locomotive when running at high speeds.

Effects on the track are being given special attention by the designers of the newer steam locomotives. For example, the "George H. Emerson" of the Baltimore & Ohio, put into service in June, 1937, has a rigid wheel base of

GIANT OF THE EMPIRE

In 1929, when these 4-8-4 "super-mountain" locomotives of the Canadian National were put into
service, they were the largest and most powerful
passenger locomotives in the British Empire. Built
at Montreal, they were intended for heavy passenger
trains on difficult grades. Motive-power development in Canada has paralleled that in the United
States more closely than that in other parts of the
British Empire. Similarity of traffic and operating
conditions in the neighbor countries has naturally
produced somewhat the same type of power,
designed to do the same sort of work.

only six feet seven inches, the distance between the centers of two pairs of driving wheels. This result was accomplished by a new departure in wheel arrangement—a 4-4-4-4 engine. The locomotive has two pairs of cylinders, each pair taking steam at 350 pounds pressure directly from the boiler to drive two pairs of driving wheels. Besides making the locomotive more flexible on curves, this arrangement, with power through two "engines" instead of one, makes possible the use of lighter reciprocating parts.

A somewhat similar arrangement of driving wheels and cylinders will feature the new "Pennsylvania Type," announced in the summer of 1937. Designed jointly by the Pennsylvania Railroad and the American, Baldwin, and Lima locomotive companies, this type is to be the most powerful high-speed reciprocating steam locomotive yet built, able to pull a train of fourteen standard passenger cars at sustained speeds of 100 miles an hour.

Practically all steam locomotives in the United States are of the reciprocating type—that is, with steam pushing the pistons back and forth in the cylinders. In marine and stationary steam-power plants, where light weight, mobility, and simplicity are not so important as they are in the locomotive, the cylinders and pistons of reciprocating engines have been replaced largely by turbines, rotating at high speed under the pressure of steam. Two major difficulties have held back the development of the turbine for railroad locomotives—the weight, size, and complications of the condenser into which the turbine must exhaust its steam; and the lack of a suitable mechanism to transmit the power from turbine to wheels. The reciprocating locomotive needs no condenser; it is coupled directly to the wheels it is to turn, without gears or intermediate drive. The fuel economy of the experimental turbine locomotives which have been operated in Sweden, England, and Germany has not appeared to be enough to counterbalance the complexities introduced.

THREE-CYLINDERED POWER

This 4-12-2 locomotive of the Union Pacific is the longest, heaviest, and most powerful steam engine in operation without an articulated "joint." Articulated or "Mallet" engines are even larger. It pulls heavy freight trains at high speed, and occasionally pulls passenger trains at sixty miles an hour. Two of the locomotive's three cylinders, placed in the usual position outside the frame of the engine, drive through main rods connected to the main driving wheels. The third cylinder, placed in the center, drives through a crank rod connected to a crank or U-bend in the front driving axle.

The Union Pacific, however, is pioneering in the building of a high-power, high-speed, condensing turbine locomotive designed to haul trains of passenger cars of standard weight at top speeds for as much as 500 miles without stops for fuel or water. The locomotive under construction will have two steam turbines of 2,500 horsepower each, which may be operated separately or together. These turbines will not be connected directly with the driving wheels but will generate electricity to drive electric motors, as in the Diesel electrics. They will be able to use the same water over and over, changing it to steam in the boiler, using the steam in the turbine, and changing the steam back to water in the condensers. Other steam turbine locomotives are in prospect, also.

Electric locomotives, drawing their power from central-station power plants, are not usual on American railroads, but where operating or traffic conditions call for them, "electrics" have been developed to haul heavier trains and haul them faster. From short boxlike units mounted on four or six driving wheels, electric engines have grown to the high-speed, heavy-duty machines which pull passenger trains between Washington and New York, at better than a mile-a-minute average speeds; or freight trains from the Potomac to the Hudson in eight hours; or the mighty units which draw transcontinental trains through the Rockies and the Cascades; or the three-unit combinations which drag great 9,000-ton trains of coal through the Virginia and West Virginia mountains.

Partly as a result of all these developments in bigger, faster engines and partly as a result of other improvements in railroad plant and equipment, the average speed of freight trains has increased within the past dozen years or so by nearly 50 per cent; the average work accomplished in each hour by 60 per cent.

72

A MODERN GIANT

This 2-10-4, the most powerful two-cylinder locomotive in service, was designed by the late W. G. Black of the Chesapeake and Ohio. Mr. Black's father designed locomotives for the Rock Island more than forty-five years ago; his grandfather designed locomotives for the old Cincinnati, Hamilton & Dayton, nearly seventy years ago. It is hard to see in the locomotives designed by the elder Blacks the ancestors of this modern giant, which hauls heavy coal trains on the Chesapeake and Ohio between the Ohio River and Lake Erie at good round speed. The engine itself weighs 566,000 pounds. With loaded tender it weighs 981,000 pounds. With the help of the booster driving on the trailing truck, it has a total tractive power of 106,584 pounds. The firebox is as big as the room of a house.

73

CHAPTER V

The Iron Horse Goes Streamlined

THE American locomotive engine is designed for work—to convert fuel into power and power into transportation service. In the story of its development there are high spots, of course—bursts of speed in a day before speed became almost commonplace; locomotive races upon the outcome of which depended matters of life and death; ceremonies to celebrate the extension of line after line of railroad as the steel net spread over the continent; historic moments, like that on the May day in 1869, when engine pilots touched at the union of East and West in the completion of the first line across the American continent. These high spots and many more there have been, but the real romance of the locomotive is in the workaday job of hauling the commerce of the continent from shore to shore in all weathers and all seasons. Its real story is one of growth and ingenious change to meet changing and ever more exacting needs.

Almost from the beginning of locomotive history there have been those who thought that this story of change and growth was about to come to an end. Nor have all those who held this opinion of the limit of possibilities of the steam locomotive been fainthearted foes of progress, by any means.

74

DESIGNED FOR "EYE APPEAL"

The "Hiawathas," pictured above, were the first modern steam locomotives designed from the ground up to be streamlined for eye appeal as well as for top speeds. Their coloring is gray, orange, and maroon. From Chicago to St. Paul and Minneapolis three railroads maintain popular and successful services with better than mile-a-minute average speed for the run of more than 400 miles. Different forms of power and different designs of trains are used by each of the three—the Diesel-electric "Zephyr" by the Burlington, the "400" standard steam train by the North Western, the specially built steam-powered "Hiawatha" by the Milwaukee Road. Such a practical test of differing types of engines and trains under severe conditions will play its part in determining the direction of railroad development.

Matthias Baldwin, who certainly could not be accused of lack of vision or imagination, announced in 1838 that his first-class engine which weighed 26,000 pounds was as heavy as would be called for and as large as he intended to build. It appeared to Mr. Baldwin then that the United States would never need a locomotive larger than this thirteen-ton model. The history of the Baldwin Locomotive Works shows to what extent Mr. Baldwin changed his mind. Recognizing changing conditions and growing needs, the designers and builders of locomotives produced the sort of power which American conditions demanded. The big locomotive was not the result of a mere desire for bigness for its own sake. It was a necessary and proper answer to American conditions, which demanded great power to handle at good speeds the heavy trains that a vast long-haul commerce at low-average freight rates made necessary.

And now, improved in performance and efficiency, locomotives have begun to change in appearance—to go streamlined. Except at speeds more extreme than are often used even on the fastest schedules, streamlining a locomotive has small effect upon the total wind-resistance of so long an object as a railroad train; but there can be no doubt of the effect of smart streamlining upon the eye of the beholder. It is a visible expression of the progress which in the past twenty years has transformed the locomotive.

As far back as the 1860's inventors were patenting sheathed locomotives, "air-splitters," and other devices to increase speed by reducing wind-resistance. More than forty years ago the Baltimore & Ohio built and operated a train designed on these principles. Thirty years ago the Union Pacific designed rail motor cars with the same idea. The idea died away because, under the conditions of operation of those days, there was no great utility in it.

But, regardless of its small utility in reducing wind-resistance, streamlining railroad equipment for appearance' sake is important. A streamlined

THE "KEEPER OF THE WINDS"

The Burlington took from Grecian mythology the name for its highly successful "Zephyr," first of the high-speed streamlined trains to use Diesel power. From the Greeks, too, comes the name for the Burlington's first stainless-steel streamlined steam locomotive, the "Aeolus." This "Keeper of the Winds" is a 4-6-4 type, engineered to run and keep on running at high speeds with a minimum of service stops, and to be easy on the track while doing it. Its pistons, pins, and rods are of exceptionally light weight, and it has roller bearings in many places where the more conventional locomotive has plain bearings. In exterior appearance it matches the "Zephyr" trains, which it is called upon to pull upon occasion in place of the Diesel-electric units regularly in service.

engine may not run any faster than one of ordinary build, but it *looks* faster —and looks count. As far back as 1928 Otto Kuhler published in the railway technical journals designs of locomotives in which this "eye-appeal" was emphasized. These designs became the basis, six years later, of the power units built by the American Locomotive Company for the famous "Hiawatha" trains of the Chicago, Milwaukee, St. Paul and Pacific Railroad. Designed as mechanical and artistic units, not only to run at top speeds of 120 miles an hour but to look as fast as they are, these pioneer engines and trains were a success right from the start, not only from the standpoint of engineering but also from that of popularity. People came down to the tracks to see them flash by.

Before the "Hiawathas" went into service, however, railroad streamlining had impressed itself upon the American public through the "Streamliner" of the Union Pacific and the Diesel-powered "Zephyr" of the Burlington— highly successful trains which became the forerunners of a numerous and increasing group of lightweight high-speed trains pulled by internal-combustion power.

In 1934 only these two small articulated streamlined trains of extreme light weight were in operation. Three years later, well above 100 trains drawn by streamlined locomotives of various sorts were running. Diesel-electric units of from 600 to 5,400 horsepower were drawing specially designed, articulated lightweight trains, specially designed semi-lightweight trains, and other trains of standard size, width, and weight in transcontinental service as well as on shorter runs. More than thirty such trains were in operation or under construction on railroads as widely distributed as the Boston and Maine, the New Haven, the Alton, the Baltimore & Ohio, the Illinois Central, the Gulf, Mobile & Northern, the Santa Fe, the Union Pacific, the Chicago & North Western,

"STREAM-STYLED"

Locomotives and trains cannot be completely streamlined because of their length and shape. They can be given smooth, flowing lines, however, which, besides reducing somewhat the resistance of the air at very high speeds, add grace and beauty to the design. This expression of the idea of speed in harmony with the power and utility of the locomotive and with the swift luxury of the train might more properly be called "stream-styling," rather than "streamlining."

the Burlington, the Rock Island, and the Southern Pacific. It is possible today to ride from coast to coast in regular service on trains pulled by Diesel power.

Power for these units is produced by a Diesel internal-combustion engine. The engine generates electricity to drive motors which in turn drive the wheels. Switching locomotives using the same principle of operation have been in successful use for a number of years, but the development of Diesels combining power and speed necessary for fast and heavy road service is still new.

The first steam locomotive to receive a streamlined sheathing was a New York Central "Hudson" type, which was converted in 1934. By 1937 nearly forty streamlined steam locomotives were in operation hauling trains for the New York Central, the Pennsylvania, the New Haven, the Milwaukee, the Burlington, the Baltimore & Ohio, and the Southern Pacific in the United States, and for the Canadian Pacific and the Canadian National in Canada.

Besides the steam locomotives and the Diesels, which make their power as they go along, an even greater number of streamlined electric passenger locomotives are now in service, operating on the Pennsylvania between New York, Philadelphia, and Washington. Others are being built for service on the New Haven Road between New York and New Haven.

Streamlining, then, is not a characteristic limited to any one form of power. Diesel electrics have it; steam engines have it; electric engines have it. Nor is efficiency, or dependability, or economy, or speed peculiar to any one form or type of power.

After somewhat more than a century of testing and growth and change, it is clear that there is no one best form of locomotive for all purposes. For each of the forms into which the "breed" of locomotives has evolved, there are uses on this vast continent. Our railroads are still testing and trying and developing all these varied forms, and are using them with success.

80